Canning And Preserving

Your Complete Guide To Canning And Preserving Food In Jars

Alex Wild

Copyright 2014 Symbol LLC

Table of Contents

Introduction

Basic Canning Methods

    Boiling Water Bath Method

    Pressure Canning Method

    Essential Canning Tips

Water Bath Canning

    What you will need

    Basic Directions

Water Bath Canning Recipes

Jams And Jellies

    Blueberry Lime Jam

    Homemade blackberry jam

    Delicious Apple Jam

    Peach jam

    Apricot jam

    Strawberry Jam

    Peach Jelly

    Creamsicle Jelly

    Basil Jelly

    Hot Jalapeno jelly

- Wild Plum Jelly
- Cranberry grape Jelly

Tasty Pickles
- Pickled beets
- Cinnamon Watermelon Rind pickles
- Dill Pickle
- Pickled peppers
- Eggplant Pickles
- Pickled Okra

Salsas
- Green tomato Salsa
- Pineapple Chili salsa
- Roasted Tomato-Chipotle Salsa
- Zesty Salsa
- Zucchini salsa

Pressure Canning
- What you will need
- Basic Directions

Meats, Fish And Poultry
- Boned Chicken
- Stew meat

- Asian Meatballs
- Smoked Fish
- Raw Venison

Delicious Soups
- Homemade Vegetable Soup
- Asparagus soup
- Black Bean Soup
- Celery Soup
- Potato Leek Soup

Canned Vegetables
- Herbed peas
- Canned Carrots
- Carrots and Peas with Chives

Conclusion

Preview Of 'Couponing For Beginners'

Our Innate Desire To Save

Introduction

I want to thank you and congratulate you for purchasing the book *"Canning And Preserving For Beginners - Your Complete Guide To Canning And Preserving Food In Jars"*.

This book contains proven steps and strategies on how to properly can and preserve your favorite foods for your enjoyment anytime you choose. If you are new to canning and preserving then don't worry as this book was made just for you. You will be on your way to being a seasoned canning expert in no time at all.

In addition to learning about canning and preserving this book also includes lots of really amazing recipes for you to get started with. I really hope you will enjoy them all!

So let's get started and have some fun!

Thanks

Alex Wild

We all want to enjoy different seasonal produce throughout the year. However, how can this be achieved? Many people have relied on supermarkets and grocery stores to provide these produce all year round although buying some produce at the supermarket when such produce is out of season can be quite expensive. So, what do you do now that it may be expensive to have fruits, jams and other produce all year round? The answer to this is definitely preservation. Preservation of food is not a new term, as early man is known to have preserved for instance his meat by salting or placing it under the sand, covering the food with sand and pouring water. This was a way of refrigeration back in the day. The good thing is that with the current technological developments, we don't have to rely on such backward ways to preserve our food.

While you can preserve food through refrigeration and drying for example, these methods may not be as effective as canning. So, what exactly is canning. Canning is a way to preserve food where the food contents are processed under high temperatures and sealed in an airtight container. The heating destroys any microorganism and the cooling creates a vacuum that no microorganism can survive. The amazing thing about canning is that it extends the shelf life of a product to between 1 year and 5 years.

Can you imagine how you can benefit from this? No need to worry about your summer fruits going bad as you can simply can them and use them over winter. Being able to stock your pantry with canned foods also cushions you against the ever-increasing prices of food. Canning is also beneficial as you know what goes into your canned food, which gives you great joy and satisfaction unlike the canned food at the supermarket that you may not be quite sure if it is a healthy option. Canning is also great fun and relatively simple. You don't need to have any specific training to learn how to can your food; some simple instructions provided in this book will be of great help in getting started with canning to preserve food.

Enough of the benefits associated with canning, let's get right into it.

Basic Canning Methods

Now that you have decided to start canning fruits, vegetables, poultry, meat etc, what is the next step? The next crucial step is to determine what home canning method to use. There are two basic home canning methods: Boiling Water Bath Method and Pressure canning method. We will look at each canning method in order for you to understand how each method is different.

Boiling Water Bath Method

This canning method is most suitable for acidic foods like most fruits, jellies, jams, fruit juices, salsas, sauerkraut and most foods that may have been added vinegar, citric acid or lemon juice. Acid foods normally contain enough acid to block the growth of bacteria and if there are any bacteria in the food, they can be destroyed quickly when heated. The boiling method is also a simple canning method and I would recommend that you first start learning the boiling canning method before you can move to the pressure canning method as this method is much easier and straightforward.

Pressure Canning Method

This canning method is most suitable for low acid foods where the bacterium Clostridium botulium can easily thrive. This kind of bacteria does not usually need oxygen; therefore, if you do not heat the low acid food to extremely high temperatures during canning and then you seal the jar, you will create the perfect environment for the bacteria to thrive and produce toxins. Some low acid foods that you could can using this method include poultry, meats and vegetables.

Essential Canning Tips

Now that you know the basic canning methods, before we move to the recipes, we need to know a few general canning tips. This is a critical part since you need to be extra careful if you will be handling water at very high degrees. You also want to do everything right to ensure that you have canned the food properly to make sure that bacteria does not grow in your canned food.

Preparation of the Food for canning

*Canning does not usually improve the quality of food; therefore, ensure that you do not use overripe fruit or poor quality food since if you start with low quality food, it will actually get worse with storage.

*No need to add more spices or seasoning to the food other than specified in the recipe as these items are usually high in bacteria and if they are in excess, they may make the canned food unsafe.

*I would also advice you not to add fat or butter unless indicated in a recipe, as these ingredients don't store well and can easily increase the rate of spoilage.

*It is also advisable not to add more low-acid ingredients like celery, peppers, onions and garlic unless specified in the recipe as such ingredients could reduce the foods acidity, which could be unsafe especially if you are using the water bath canning method.

*Only use " clear-jel" to thicken your recipes and don't use starches, rice, flour, pasta or barley as such items will absorb the liquid during the heating process and slow how the food heats up, which could lead to under-processing and unsafe food.

*When making sweet preserves like jam, add the amount of sugar as indicated in the recipe to the fruit at once, as it helps the mixture jel properly.

*Don't double recipes as recipes are tested as written. Instead of doubling the recipe, you can opt to make two batches.

*If you want to make a food more acidic by adding lemon juice, it is more preferable to use bottled lemon juice since fresh lemon juice varies in acidity and this could threaten the safety of the food.

*Some cut or peeled fruits darken when exposed to air. You can put the cut fruits in 1 teaspoon of ascorbic acid and 1 gallon of water. You can also put the fruits in lemon juice solution (1-gallon water and ¾-cup lemon juice).

*If you are canning more than one type of food, ensure that you clean your utensils like knives and boards before you move from canning one food to the other.

Heating process during canning

*Never process the jars in any oven whether gas, electric or microwave. Steam canning is also not broadly recommended.

*Ensure to increase water-bath processing time in case of altitudes of 1000 feet and more to compensate for the lower temperature of boiling at high altitudes. Below is a chart that will be useful as you start home canning.

Altitude Adjustment chart

Pressure canning method

Pressure canners would require an additional ½ pound pressure for every 1000 feet above sea level.

Adjustment for Pressure Canner		
Altitude in Feet	Dial Gauge Canner	Weighted Gauge Canner
0-1000	10	10
1001-2000	11	15
2001-4000	12	15
4001-6000	13	15
6001-8000	14	15
8000-10,000	15	15

Water Bath Canning Method

This method requires an additional two minutes for every 1000 ft above sea level.

Altitude Adjustments for Boiling Water Bath Canner	
Altitude in Feet	Increase processing time
1001-3000	5 minutes
3001-6000	10 minutes
6001-8000	15 minutes
8001-10,000	20 minutes

Equipment and Tools used for canning

*Always use the size of the jar specified in the recipe. Avoid using large jars than specified as this could easily result in an unsafe product especially since the recipe is meant to fit perfectly in a particular jar and thus using a larger jar would mean that the headspace left will be much larger.

*To remove hard water films or scale on jars, soak them for several hours in a solution of 1 gallon of water and 1 cup vinegar.

*When canning, ensure that you have a clean towel to wipe the rim to avoid any food remaining on the jar. When one side of the towel gets dirty, use another clean part.

Water Bath Canning

As earlier indicated, this canning method is most suitable for highly acidic foods. We will look at what you need when using this canning method and a basic procedure to follow.

What you will need

Canning jars with metal rings and seals

Jar-lifting tongs

Water-bath canner with internal rack

Canning funnel

Wooden chopstick to stir contents with

Bowls, pots, spoons and measuring cups for the cooking preparation

Lid-lifting tongs

Slotted spoon and long-handled spoon

Food to be canned

Thermometers for testing water and food temperatures

Clean dishtowels for wiping the jars

Clean dishtowels for placing the jars for cooling

Marker and labels

Timer or Watch

Basic Directions

Step 1

The first thing you need to do is to sterilize all your equipment. You can do this by washing the equipment, by steaming the lids and jars or dunking them in simmering water for around 15 minutes. You can then start removing the jars and lids from the simmering water one at a time and line them on a clean work surface when ready to fill the jars.

Step 2

The next step is to prepare the food. Different recipes will require you to prepare the food differently. Some recipes may require you to blanch food in which case you will place the food in hot water or boiling water for a certain amount of time after which you remove and place in cool water to stop the cooking process. Other recipes may require you to precook the food then hot pack them into the jars. Simply follow what the recipe indicates. I will provide some recipes later on to help you understand this much better.

Step 3

The next step is to fill the prepared food into your jars ensuring that you leave the required amount of headspace between the food and the lid. Normally the specific recipe will indicate the amount of headspace that is necessary.

Step 4

Remove any air bubbles in the jar by stirring with the chopstick. Once you have gotten rid of the air bubbles, you can set the lid on the jar's rim and twist the band until it resists. Remember not to over tighten.

Step 5

Fill the canner with water to almost the top and bring it to a boil. Place the jars in the rack and allow the water to return to a boil. Ensure that the jars are covered with an inch of the water. For processing times of over 30 minutes, ensure that the jars are covered with two inches of water, meaning that you may have to add some water if the water falls below this and maintain a steady boil. Once the water returns to a boil, you can begin timing depending on the recipe.

Step 6

After boiling, turn off the heat and remove the water canner lid. Do not remove the jars until five minutes have elapsed. After five minutes, use a jar lifter to place the jars on a towel at least two inches between them. Allow the jars to sit undisturbed at room temperature for about 12-24 hours. In order to know if the jars have sealed properly, if the lid flexes up and down, note that the jar has not been sealed properly.

Step 7

Remove the metal rings as they can corrode during storage. You may also reuse the metal rings. Label the contents and date clearly, and store your canned food in your pantry.

Water Bath Canning Recipes

Jams And Jellies

Blueberry Lime Jam
Yields: Around 6 half-pints

What you will need

4 ½ cups blueberries

1/3 cup lime juice

1 tablespoon lime zest

5 cups of sugar

1 package dry pectin

6 (8 oz) jars

Instructions

Crush the blueberries and combine these with pectin in a large pot.

Bring the mixture to a boil as you stir frequently. Add sugar and stir until all sugar has dissolved.

Stir in the lime juice and grated lime peel and return to a rolling boil then boil for another 1 minute as you stir constantly and remove from heat then skim foam if necessary and ladle the jam into hot jars ensuring to leave a quarter headspace. Adjust the caps appropriately.

Place the jars in a boiling water canner for 15 minutes then remove after the 15 minutes elapse to cool.

Homemade blackberry jam
Yield: Makes 6 half pint jars

What you will need

5 cups crushed black berries

1 (1 ¾ ounce) package dry pectin

7 cups of sugar

6 (8 oz) jars

Instructions

Put the berries in a large pot (around 8 qt). Add the pectin to the berries slowly as you continue stirring constantly.

Heat on high as you continue stirring until the mixture comes to a full boil then add all the sugar and continue stirring. Boil for an additional 1 minute, then ladle the jam into 8 oz jars making sure to leave ¼ inch head space.

Wipe the rim of the jam and put canning lids and rings on.

Put the jars in a canner with very hot water ensuring that the water is 1 inch above the jars and process in boiling water bath for around ten minutes.

Remove from the boiling water and set them on a towel to cool for around 12 hours.

Delicious Apple Jam
Yields: About 6 half pints

What you will need

6 cups, peeled and chopped Granny Smith Apples

2 cups unsweetened apple juice

Juice and zest of 1 lemon

1 teaspoon ground cinnamon

3 tablespoons pectin

1 ½ cups sugar

¾ cup raisins

6 (8 oz) jars

Instructions

Prepare the boiling water canner. Heat the jars in simmering water and not boiling water until when you are ready to use them. Wash the lids with warm soapy water and put the bands aside.

Combine the apples, lemon juice and peel in a large pan. Bring to a boil, reduce the heat and simmer until the apples start to soften then remove from heat and whisk in the pectin and then add the cinnamon and raisins and return the mixture to a boil. Boil for five minutes, remove from heat and stir in the sugar then skim the foam if necessary.

Ladle the jam into hot jars ensuring to leave ¼ inch head space. Wipe rim, put the lid at the center then put the bands and tighten to fingertip tight.

Process the jars in boiling water for ten minutes as you adjust for altitude. Remove the jars, cool and check if the lids are properly sealed. Ensure that lids do not flex up and down when the center is pressed.

Peach jam
Yields: 6 half pints

What you will need

5 lbs peaches

5 cups sugar

3 teaspoons lemon juice

6 (8 oz) jars

Instructions

Place all ingredients in a large glass bowl and allow it to stand for 1 hour. Transfer these ingredients to an enamel pot. Bring to a full boil and boil for 25 minutes to reach the jell point. Stir constantly as the mixtures nears the jell point.

Skim off foam if necessary and ladle into clean hot jars ensuring you leave ¼-inch headspace.

Process the jars in boiling water for ten minutes. Remove and set on a towel to cool for 12 hours.

Apricot jam
Yields: 6 half pints

What you will need

3 ½ cups finely chopped apricots

13- oz liquid pectin

5 ¾ cups sugar

1/3 cup lemon juice

6 (8 oz) glass jars with lids and bands

Instructions

Prepare boiling water canner and heat jars in hot water until when you want to ladle the jam into the jars. Also, wash lids in warm soapy water.

Combine the lemon juice, apricots and sugar in a pan. Bring the mixture to a boil while stirring frequently.

Immediately add pectin and continue to hard-boil for another minute as you stir constantly. Remove from heat and skim if needed.

Ladle your hot jam into the prepared jars making sure that you leave ¼-inch headspace. Wipe the rim clean put the lid and apply the band until tight.

Strawberry Jam
Yield: 6 half pints

What you will need

5 cups crushed strawberries

7 cups granulated sugar

¼ cup lemon juice

6 tablespoons classic pectin

8 (8 oz) half pint glass jars

Instructions

Prepare the boiling water canner.

Combine lemon juice and strawberries in a pan and stir in the pectin gradually. Bring the mixture to a rolling boil, over heat and stir constantly.

Add sugar as you stir constantly to dissolve then return mixture to a boil. Boil hard for 1 minute, stirring constantly. Remove from heat then skim off if necessary.

Immediately put the jam into the jars making sure to leave a quarter inch headspace then wipe rim, put the lid on the jar and apply band until tight.

Process in boiling water canner for ten minutes. Remove jars, cool and check if the lids are properly sealed.

Peach Jelly
Yield: Makes 1 ¼ pints

What you will need

2 tablespoons powdered pectin

4 peaches, sliced

5 bags green tea

2 cups water

2 cups sugar

Instructions

Prepare two ½ pint jars and one ¼ pint jar.

Combine the water and sugar in a large pot, bring to a simmer and stir until all sugar is dissolved. Add four tea bags to a pot and allow them to simmer for five minutes.

Once the five minutes are over, remove the tea bags and add the sliced peaches. Let this simmer for around ten minutes, as you taste frequently to determine the intensity of the flavor. Once you achieve a suitable balance of green tea and peach tastes, strain liquid though a fine mesh sieve making sure to press the peaches to get as much liquid as possible.

Return this syrup to pot and add two tablespoons of powdered pectin. Bring this to a rapid boil and monitor temperature. Once the jelly liquid reaches approximately 220 degrees, it is ready.

Turn off the heat and transfer jelly into the jars. Make sure that you wipe the rims of the jars, put the lids and rings and put in boiling water bath for ten minutes.

Once the time elapses, turn off the heat and remove the jars from canner, put them on a towel for them to cool. Once the jars cool, you can remove the rings and test seal then store appropriately.

Creamsicle Jelly
Yields: 2 pints

Ingredients

4 cups fresh orange juice

2 vanilla beans, split and scraped

4 cups sugar

1 packet liquid pectin

Instructions

Combine vanilla bean scrapings and beans, sugar and orange juice in a large pot. Bring to a boil over high heat and cook with intention of reducing volume to around half.

Use a thermometer to track the temperature and once you get to 220 degrees and able to maintain the temperature even after stirring, add the pectin and cook for another 2-3 minutes then remove from the heat.

Remove vanilla beans from pot and pour the jelly into prepared jars. Wipe the rims and put the lids and bands adequately.

Proceed to put the jars boiling water canner for around 10 minutes. Once the time is up, you can remove the jars from the pot, put on a countertop lined with towels, and allow the jars to cool. Once they have cooled, you can check the seals and store unsealed jars in the fridge and the rest in your pantry.

Basil Jelly
Yields: 3-4 half pints

Ingredients

1 ½ cups crushed fresh basil leaves

3 cups apple juice

2 drops green food coloring

1 (6-ounce) packet liquid pectin

3 ½ cups sugar

2 tablespoons cider vinegar

Instructions

Bring one cup of apple juice to a rolling boil, pour over crushed basil leaves and let this rest for 25 minutes.

Strain the liquid into a pan, add the other two cups of ACV and green food coloring and stir to mix.

Bring to a hard boil, stir in pectin and sugar, return to a hard boil, as you stir constantly, and cook until a jelly point is achieved.

Remove from heat, skim off the foam and remove the leaves from the jelly using a slotted spoon.

Pour the mixture into half-pint jars leaving ½-inch headroom at the top.

Attach the lids, bands, and process for 15 minutes in a water bath canner. Remove from the canner and cool on a towel placed on the counter.

Once cool, check seals and refrigerate any that may have not been sealed properly. Remove the bands from the others and store in a cool dry place.

Hot Jalapeno jelly
Yield: 7 half pints

Ingredients

2 jalapeno peppers, seeded and chopped

1 ½ cups white vinegar, divided

3 medium green peppers, cut into 1-inch pieces, divided

2 pouches (3 ounce each) liquid fruit pectin

½ to 1 teaspoon cayenne pepper

About 6 drops green food coloring optional

6 ½ cups sugar

Instructions

Place half the green peppers, jalapenos and ½ cup vinegar in food processor and blend until pureed. Transfer to a large pan. Repeat the same with the remaining green peppers and the other ½ cup vinegar.

Add sugar, remaining vinegar and cayenne to pan and bring to a boil over high heat while making sure that you stir constantly. Quickly stir in pectin and return the mixture to a rolling boil. Boil for one minute as you stir constantly.

Remove from heat, skim off foam if necessary and add the food coloring. Ladle the mixture into hot ½ pint jars making sure to leave ¼ inch headspace. Remove any air bubbles using a wooden chopstick if necessary then put the lids and adjust the bands until tight.

Process for ten minutes in a boiling water canner. Remove once time elapses and place on a counter top with kitchen towels to allow it to cool.

Wild Plum Jelly
Yield: 8 half pints

Ingredients

5 pounds wild plums, pitted and halved

7 ½ cups sugar

1 package (1 ¾ ounces) powdered fruit pectin

4 cups water

Instructions

Simmer water and plums until the plums are tender; should take around thirty minutes. Strain the plum mixture through a cheesecloth and allow this mixture to stand for 30 minutes or until the liquid measures around 5 ½ cups.

Return this liquid to the pan, add pectin and stir then bring to a boil. Add the sugar then bring to a rolling boil. Boil for around 1 minute as you stir constantly.

Remove from heat, skim off any foam and carefully ladle the hot mixture into hot sterilized half- pint jars ensuring that you leave ¼ inch headspace. If any air bubbles are present, remove using a chopstick then put the lids and bands and adjust the band until tight.

Process for 5 minutes in boiling water canner. Remove to cool once the five minutes elapse and check if well sealed then store in a cool dry place.

Cranberry grape Jelly
Yield: 6 half pints

Ingredients

¾ cup fresh grape juice

2 cups fresh cranberry juice

3 ¼ cups white sugar

1 (2- ounce) package dry pectin

Instructions

Pour the grape and cranberry juices into a pot. Add pectin and stir until well dissolved. Bring mixture to a boil over high heat and stir in sugar then allow it to boil for one minute as you stir constantly.

Remove from heat, skim off any form and pour the jelly into hot jars making sure to leave ¼ inch headspace. Adjust the lids and process for ten minutes in a boiling water bath.

Remove from the bath and place on a towel to cool. Once cooled, you can check if the jars are properly sealed then store in a cool dry place.

Tasty Pickles

Pickled beets
Yield: 6 half pints

Ingredients

6 quarts of fresh beets

2 cups water

2 cups sugar

2 cups cider vinegar

1 teaspoon whole cloves

2 cinnamon sticks

Instructions

Wash the beets and put them in a pot then pour water to cover the beets then boil for 20 minutes.

Drain and cool in cold water, remove ends, peel and cut into quarters.

Bring the remaining ingredients to a boil, then add the beets and simmer for around ten minutes. Remove the cinnamon sticks and pack in hot jars, seal and put the jars in hot water bath for ten minutes.

Remove and allow to cool then store in a cool dry place.

Cinnamon Watermelon Rind pickles
Yield: 4 to 5 pints

What you will need

16 cups peeled, sliced watermelon rind

6 cups granulated sugar

1 cup pickling salt

3 cinnamon sticks broken in half

4 cups white vinegar

8 cups cool water, divided

4 pint glass jars with lids and bands

Instructions

Day 1:

Layer the watermelon rind and salt in a large bowl, add 4 cups of cool water and place a large inverted plate on top of the rind in order to try to push it down. Cover with plastic wrap and refrigerate for 8 hours.

Day 2

Transfer the rind to a colander, drain, and rinse in cool running water.

Combine the rinds with the remaining 4 cups of cool water in a large pan. Bring to a boil and reduce the heat to allow it to boil until rind is tender when you test using a fork. This should take you around 10 minutes. Drain and set aside.

Mix cinnamon sticks, vinegar and sugar in a large pan. Bring to a boil over medium heat and stir to dissolve the sugar.

Reduce the heat and boil gently for five minutes or until the cinnamon has infused the liquid. Add the drained rind and return to a boil. Reduce heat and boil gently as you stir occasionally for an hour or until the watermelon rind becomes translucent then discard the cinnamon sticks.

Prepare the boiling water canner and heat jars in simmering water. Pack the hot rind into hot jars ensuring that you leave ½ inch headroom. Ladle the hot pickling liquid into the jar to cover the rind making sure to leave half an inch headroom. Wipe rim and put a lid on jar, put the band and tighten until tight. Put the jars in a boiling water bath for ten minutes.

Remove jars and cool then check the lids for seal after 24 hours.

Dill Pickle
Yields: 6 (16 oz) pints

What you will need

Green or dry dill (1 head for every jar)

4 lbs pickling cucumbers

2 tablespoons salt

3 cups sugar

2 tablespoons mixed pickling spice

6 cups vinegar

6 (16 oz) pint glass jars with lids and bands

Instructions

Prepare the boiling water canner and heat the jars in simmering water until when you want to use them.

Wash cucumbers, drain and cut into ¼-inch thick slices ensuring to discard the ends.

Combine the vinegar, salt and sugar in a large pan. Tie the spices in a spice bag and add vinegar to the mixture. Bring to a boil and reduce heat then simmer for 15 minutes. Keep hot until when you want to use then remove the spice bag.

Pack the cucumbers into the hot jars making sure to leave ½ inch headspace and put one head of dill in each jar.

Ladle the liquid over the cucumbers making sure to leave ½ inch headspace. Wipe the rim if necessary and center the lid on jar, apply the band and adjust accordingly.

Process the jars in boiling water canner for 15 minutes making sure to adjust for altitude.

Remove the jars and cool. Check if the jars are properly sealed after 24 hours then store in a cool dry place if well sealed.

Pickled peppers
Makes 4 (16 oz) pints

What you will need

20 medium sweet red peppers, peeled, seeded, deveined and cut lengthwise

½ cup water

1 ½ cups dry white wine

1 ½ cups white vinegar

½ cup granulated sugar

4 cloves garlic, roasted and skin removed then mashed

1 ½ cups cider vinegar

2 tablespoons dried oregano

1 cup chopped onion

4 teaspoons pickling salt

4 (16 oz) pint glass jars with bands and lids

Instructions

Roast garlic cloves and pepper on a grill until charred making sure to roast all sides. Once the skin of the peppers chars and garlic has charred spots, you can remove from heat and place peppers in a paper bag until cool enough to handle then remove the skins. Squeeze the roasted garlic cloves to remove the peel.

Combine the roasted garlic, cider vinegar, white vinegar, water, white wine, sugar, onion, salt and oregano in a large pan and bring to a boil. Stir to dissolve the sugar then remove from heat and boil gently for five minutes or until the oregano and garlic flavors are infused into the liquid.

Pack the peppers into the jars making sure that you leave half an inch headroom and ladle the pickling liquid into the jar to cover the peppers making sure to leave ½ inch headspace. You may remove any air bubbles if necessary, wipe clean the rim, put the lid at the center of the jar and apply band tightly.

Process jars in a boiling water canner for 15 minutes. Remove the jars and cool then check lids if well sealed after 24 hours.

Eggplant Pickles
Yield: 6 (16 oz) pints

What you will need

5lb eggplant

1 ½ cups white vinegar

4 ½ cups cold water

6 cloves garlic

1 tablespoon oregano leaves

3 tablespoons granulated sugar

½ cup balsamic vinegar

2 teaspoon pickling salt

6 (16 oz) jars

Instructions

Bring a pot of water to a boil, remove the ends of the eggplant and peel. Cut the eggplant into 3-inch thick pieces and drop these pieces into the boiling water. Boil for ten minutes while pressing the eggplant under the water frequently to remove any air.

Carefully drain the eggplant and cover with cold water, drain thoroughly.

Mix the oregano, sugar, 4 ½ cups of water and vinegars in a large pan. Cover and bring to a boil.

Place 1 clove garlic in each hot jar then fill the jar with eggplant making sure to leave ½-inch headspace. Using a wooden chopstick remove any air bubbles, wipe rim and center the lid on jar then apply band and tighten.

Process jars in boiling water canner for 15 minutes. Remove jars and cool. Check the lids for seal after 24 hours and store in a cool dry place if properly sealed.

Pickled Okra
Yield: 3 (32 oz) quarts jars

What you will need

3 lbs okra

3 garlic cloves

3 hot chilies

1 tablespoon mustard seed

¼ cup kosher salt

1 quart cider vinegar

3 sprigs fresh dill

3 (32 oz) quarts jars

Instructions

Bring vinegar, mustard seed, 1 ½ cups water and salt to a boil in a small pot. Turn off heat and divide the chilies, dill, garlic and okra between the three jars. Pack tightly and ensure that you leave ¼-inch headspace.

Pour the hot brine into the jars making sure to leave ¼ inch headspace. Adjust the lid and tighten the canning band.

Process jars in boiling water bath canner for ten minutes. Remove canner lid and wait for five minutes before you can remove the jars.

Check lids for seal after 24 hours.

Salsas

Green tomato Salsa
Yield: 6 (8 oz) pints

What you will need

7 cups chopped cored and peeled green tomatoes

2 cups chopped red onion

5 to 10 jalapeno

2 cloves garlic, chopped

½ cup loosely packed cilantro

½ cup lime juice

1 teaspoon salt

1 teaspoon dried oregano

2 teaspoons ground cumin

6 half pint glass jars

Instructions

Combine the onion, peppers, tomatoes, lime juice and garlic in a pan. Bring to a boil and stir in cumin, cilantro, salt and pepper and oregano. Reduce the heat and simmer for 5 minutes.

Ladle the hot salsa into hot jars making sure that you leave half an inch headroom. You can then get rid of, wipe clean the rim and put a hot lid on the jar then apply the band and adjust accordingly.

Process the filled jars in a boiling water canner for 20 minutes. Remove the jars and let them cool. Check lids for seal after 24 hours.

Pineapple Chili salsa
Yield: 6 (8 oz) half pints

What you will need

4 cups seeded, peeled papaya

1 cup golden raisins

2 cups cubed, cored and peeled pineapple

½ cup pineapple juice

½ cup seeded and chopped Anaheim peppers

1 cup lemon juice

2 tablespoons chopped cilantro

2 tablespoons chopped green onion

2 tablespoons packed brown sugar

½ cup lime juice

6 (8 oz) half pint glass jars

Instructions

Prepare boiling water canner and heat jars in simmering water until ready to use.

Combine the pineapple, papaya, lemon juice, raisins, pineapple juice, lime juice, green onion, peppers, brown sugar and cilantro in a pan. Bring to a boil as you stir constantly. Reduce heat and boil as you stir frequently until thickened, about ten minutes.

Ladle hot salsa into the jars leaving half an inch headspace. Proceed to get rid of any air bubbles using a wooden chopstick then seal using your lid and band.

Check lids for seal after 12 hours then store in a cool dry place.

Roasted Tomato-Chipotle Salsa
Yield: 6 (16 oz) pints

What you will need

12 dried chipotle chili peppers

2 lbs husked tomatillos

1 teaspoon salt

1 cup white vinegar

2 teaspoons sugar

2 small onions

2 lbs plum tomatoes

6 (16 oz) glass jars

1 head garlic, broken into cloves

12 dried cascabel chili peppers

Instructions

Toast the cascabel and chipotle chilies in a dry skillet over medium heat until they release their aroma and become pliable. Transfer to a large bowl then add two cups of hot water. Weigh the chilies in a bowl and weight it down to ensure they remain submerged. Let them soak until softened then transfer the chilies to a blender and puree until smooth.

Roast tomatoes, tomatillos, garlic and onions under a broiler ensuring to turn to roast all sides until the tomatoes and tomatillos are softened, blackened and blistered and onions and garlic are blackened in spots, about 15 minutes. Set the garlic and onions aside in order to cool. Place the tomatoes and tomatillos in paper bags. Secure openings and put aside until cool enough to handle. Peel the onions, tomatoes, garlic and then chop the garlic and onion and set aside.

Puree roasted tomatoes and tomatillos and the reserved chilies until smooth in a food processor then put aside.

Combine the tomatillo puree, roasted garlic and onion, sugar, salt and vinegar in a large pan. Bring to a boil while stirring constantly. Reduce heat and boil while stirring frequently until thickened.

Ladle the hot salsa into jars leaving ½" inch headroom. Wipe the rim clean and put the lid and band and adjust until tight.

Process filled jars in a boiling water canner for around 15 minutes, adjusting for altitude. Remove jars and cool then check lids to ensure that they are properly sealed.

Zesty Salsa
Yield: Makes 6 (16 oz) pints

What you will need

10 cups chopped, cored and peeled tomatoes

5 cups chopped onions

5 cups chopped seeded green bell peppers

1 ¼ cups cider vinegar

1 tablespoon salt

2 tablespoons finely chopped cilantro

2 ½ cups chili peppers, chopped

3 cloves garlic, finely chopped

1 teaspoon hot pepper sauce

6 (16 oz) pint glass jars

Instructions

Combine green peppers, tomatoes, vinegar, chili peppers, cilantro, garlic, hot pepper sauce, salt and onions in a large pan. Bring to a boil while stirring constantly then reduce the heat and boil gently until slightly thickened.

Ladle the salsa into hot jars ensuring that there is headroom left of around half an inch. You can then get rid of any air bubbles and adjust headspace then wipe the jar rim, put the lid accordingly on the jar and put the band until tight.

Process the jars in a boiling water canner for 15 minutes. Once the 15 minutes have elapsed, remove the jars and cool. Check lids for seal after 12 hours then store in a cool dry place if sealed properly.

Zucchini salsa
Yield: 10-12 pints

Ingredients

2 tablespoons dry mustard

10 cups zucchini, peeled and shredded

4 onions, chopped

1 tablespoon garlic powder

1 tablespoon pickling salt

2 red peppers, chopped

1 tablespoon cumin

2 tablespoons red pepper flakes

1 cup brown sugar

12 ounces tomato paste

5 cups chopped ripe tomatoes

2 cups white vinegar

1 teaspoon nutmeg

2 tablespoons cornstarch

1 teaspoon pepper

¼ cup pickling salt

2 green peppers, chopped

Instructions

Day 1:

Combine onions, zucchini, red pepper, green pepper and salt in a large bowl, mix and let it stand for one night.

Day 2:

Rinse and drain well the mixture into a large pot then add garlic, mustard, vinegar, cumin brown sugar, pepper flakes, nutmeg, salt, cornstarch, 1 tablespoon salt, tomato paste and tomatoes.

Bring to a boil and simmer for around 15 minutes then pour into sterilized jars and seal.

Process the jars in a water bath for 15 minutes and store appropriately if well sealed.

Pressure Canning

Pressure canning is most suitable for canning low acidic foods like meats, poultry, fish and vegetables. This is due to some bacteria being able to survive in low acid foods; hence, the need to heat the food to extreme temperatures to get rid of the bacteria.

What you will need

Pressure canner

Jar lifter

Glass jars and lids

Funnel

Wooden spoon

Ladle

Hot jar handle

Food to be canned

Basic Directions

Remember that different recipes will call for different instructions. What I have provided here is a basic guideline on how pressure canning works.

Step 1

Inspect your jars to ensure that they don't have cracks, nicks, rims or sharp edges as this can easily cause breakages during the heating. Wash the canning jars and lids in hot soapy water, rinse and dry. Heat the jars until you are ready to heat them.

This is important to avoid breakages especially when packing the jars with hot food. In addition, the heating aids in sterilizing the equipment. Remember however not to heat the lids; leave them at room temperature to allow for easy handling.

Step 2

Prepare the pressure canner by adding around two to three inches of water and bring to a simmer over medium heat. Always ensure that the water remains at a simmer in the pressure canner until you are ready to put the jars filled with food in the pressure canner.

Step 3

Prepare the food for filling according to the specific recipe you are using.

Step 4

Once the food is ready, remove the jars from the hot water using a jar lifter ensuring that you empty any water that may be in the jars. Pour the prepared food into the jars with the use of a jar funnel ensuring to leave head space as recommended by your recipes. Using a wooden spoon, remove air bubbles to ensure adequate headspace as any air bubbles trapped would come at the top during processing and interfere with the canning process.

Step 5

Use a clean damp cloth to wipe the jar rim to remove any food residue. Then place the lids on the jars and close ensuring that you don't close too tightly. Place the jars in the pressure canner and when done placing, ensure that there is at least an inch or two of water above the jars.

Step 6

Ensure that the vent pipe on the canner is open and lock the lid then adjust heat to medium high. Allow the steam to escape through the vent pipe ensuring a steady flow of steam is escaping. Allow the steam to escape and vent for around ten minutes until only steam is coming out of the pipe. After the 10 minutes, you can adjust heat according to the specific recipe pressure.

Step 7

Once you have processed the jars according to the specific pressure, remove the canner from the heat and leave the weighted gauge on. Allow the canner to rest at room temperature until the pressure is at zero. Remove the weight, unlock lid ensuring to tilt it away to avoid scolding with steam then remove the jars carefully from the pressure canner and place them on a towel ensuring to leave around two inches space between the jars. Allow the jars to sit undisturbed for around 24 hours.

Step 8

Check the jar lids thoroughly to see if they are well sealed. If within 24 hours, the lid does not seal adequately, refrigerate immediately. Clean the jars and lids using a damp towel and store appropriately depending on the recipe.

Meats, Fish And Poultry

Boned Chicken

What you will need

Chicken

Salt

Water Glass preserving jars with bands and lids

Instructions

Prepare the pressure canner and sterilize the jars and lids.

Steam or boil the chicken until it is about 2/3 done then remove skin and bones.

Pack the hot chicken into the hot jars ensuring that you leave 1 inch headspace. Add a teaspoon of salt to each quart jar.

Ladle the chicken broth over the chicken leaving around 1-inch headspace and remove air bubbles.

Wipe the rim, center the hot lid, apply the band and adjust accordingly until it is fingertip tight.

Process the jars in a pressure canner at 10 pounds pressure for 75 minutes for pints and 90 minutes for quarts.

Once the time elapses, remove the jars and let them cool on a towel-lined counter. Check the lids for proper sealing then store in a cool dry place if well sealed.

Stew meat

What you will need

Lamb, Beef, Mutton, Venison or Pork

Water

Glass jars with lids and bands

Instructions

Prepare the pressure canner and heat the jars in simmering water until when you want to use them.

Cut the meat into 1 ½ - 2 inch cubes to remove the fat.

Put the meat in a large saucepan and cover with water. Simmer the meat until it is hot throughout then pack hot meat into the jars leaving an inch of headspace. Add a teaspoon of salt to each quart jar.

Ladle hot cooking liquid over the meat leaving an inch headspace. Remove the air bubbles and wipe the rim appropriately. Center the hot lid on the jar, apply the band and adjust accordingly.

Process the jars in a pressure canner at 10 pounds of pressure for 75 minutes for pints and 90 minutes for quarts as you adjust the altitude appropriately.

Remove from pressure canner once the time elapses and allow to cool on a towel. Check jars to ensure that they are properly sealed and store in your pantry.

Asian Meatballs

Ingredients

3 lbs lean ground turkey

5 cloves garlic, grated

5 green onions chopped

2 tablespoons soy sauce

1 teaspoon garlic powder

5 tablespoons Teriyaki Ginger sauce

1 teaspoon freshly ground pepper

3 teaspoons salt

2 inch fresh ginger grated

Instructions

Combine all the ingredients in a bowl and mix well using your hands. Make patties depending on the size of meatballs.

Spray a baking sheet with non-stick cooking spray and line the meatballs on the baking sheet.

Bake for 350°F for around 45 minutes until almost done. Pack the hot jars with the cooked meatballs and add chicken stock making sure to leave an inch of headspace, remove air bubbles, wipe the rim and adjust the lid.

Process the jars in a pressure can for 75 minutes for pints at 10 pounds pressure for weighted gauge and 11 pounds for dial gauge.

Once the processing time elapses, remove from the pressure can and allow cooling for 12-24 hours then check if the jars are properly sealed.

Smoked Fish

Ingredients

Lightly smoked Fish

Instructions

Cut the fish into pieces that can fit into the jar, add 4 quarts of water to the pressure canner.

Pack the fish into hot jars making sure to leave 1 inch headspace. Wipe rims and place the canning lids.

Process the jars in a pressure canner for 110 minutes and 10 pounds of pressure for pints.

Remove once the processing time elapses and allow for cooling. Make sure to check whether the jars and well sealed.

Raw Venison

Ingredients

Venison

Canning salt

Instructions

Remove any bruised areas and excess fat then slice across the grain into an inch thick slices or cubes but ensure that the lengths fit into the jars.

Pack the meat into hot jars making sure to leave an inch headspace. Add canning salt if necessary; around two teaspoons is enough per quart. No need to add any liquid.

Remove air bubbles if any, wipe the rims, place the lids and screw bands on finger tight.

Place jars in a pressure canner ensuring that the jars don't touch each other. Process for 75 minutes for pints and 90 minutes for quarts.

Once the time elapses, place on a towel to cool then store in your pantry.

Delicious Soups

Homemade Vegetable Soup
Yield: 7 (32 oz) quarts

Ingredients

8 cups tomatoes, peeled, cored and chopped

6 cups ¾- inch sliced carrots

6 cups peeled and cubed potatoes

2 cups 1-inch sliced celery

4 cups uncooked corn kernels

4 cups green lima beans

6 cups water

2 cups chopped onions

Salt and pepper to taste

Instructions

Prepare pressure canner and heat jars in simmering water until ready for use. Combine vegetables in a large pot, add water and bring to a boil. Reduce heat and simmer for 5 minutes then season with salt and pepper if necessary.

Ladle hot soup into hot jars making sure to leave an inch headspace. Make sure that you get rid of any air bubbles, wipe the rim clean of any spilt food and center the lid on jar then apply band and adjust until it fits.

Process filled jars in a pressure canner at 10 pounds pressure for 55 minutes for pints and 85 minutes for quarts.

Remove jars and cool then check lids for seal after 12 hours. Ensure that the lids do not flex up and down if you press the center.

Asparagus soup

Ingredients

3 lbs fresh asparagus

1 cup minced shallots

8 cups chicken broth

½ teaspoon salt

¼ teaspoon ground white pepper

1 tablespoon minced garlic

Instructions

Sterilize the jars and keep them in hot water until ready to use.

Use a tiny amount of olive oil to sauté the garlic and shallots until translucent. Heat the beef stock over medium heat and remove from heat.

Fill the jars with asparagus ¾ full and add about ¼ cup garlic/shallot and equal portion of pepper and salt. Once you have filled the jars, add hot stock and leave ¼ inch headroom. If necessary remove air bubbles and refill to maintain the appropriate headspace. Wipe the rims of the jars to remove any food particles then center the lids and adjust the band to "finger tight".

Place the cans in the pressure canner, lock the lid and then bring the canner to a boil. Vent steam for ten minutes then close the vent by adding the pressure regulator.

Process pints at 10lbs of pressure for 75 minutes. Once the process is complete, turn off the heat and let the pressure get to zero. Wait two or more minutes before you open the vent.

Remove the canner lid and wait for another ten minutes before you remove jars then place on a dishtowel in a place that they will sit overnight to cool.

Black Bean Soup
Ingredients

1 lb dried black beans

4 carrots diced

2 onions, one halved and one finely diced

1 pablano pepper, seeded and diced

3 clove garlic, minced

2 cups ham diced

2 ½ quarts chicken stock

2 teaspoons ground cumin

1 ½ teaspoons freshly ground black pepper

3 teaspoons kosher salt

2 teaspoons oregano

½ teaspoon cayenne pepper

Instructions

Sort and wash the beans then soak them overnight in a bowl with enough water to cover by around 3 inches

Drain beans, rinse then put in a pot then cover with cold water up to 3 inches. Add the onion that is cut in half, bring to a boil then reduce the heat and simmer for around 30 minutes.

Combine chicken stock, vegetables and spices in another pot and allow to simmer for five minutes until heated through.

Strain the beans and discard the onion and liquid. Strain the stock and reserve the stock and vegetable.

In a hot jar, fill ¼ full of the beans, ¼ cup ham and vegetables and add stock making sure to leave 1 inch headspace. Remove air bubbles, wipe rim and put the hot lid.

Place the jars in a pressure canner and process quarts for 90 minutes and pints for 75 minutes at 11 on dial gauge or 10 lbs pressure.

Celery Soup

Ingredients

1 lb celery, finely diced

1 onion, finely diced

1 clove garlic minced

¼ cup dry white wine

1 quart vegetable or chicken stock

1 tablespoon olive oil

1 russet potato, peeled and diced

Instructions

In a Dutch oven, sauté in 1 tablespoon olive oil the onions until translucent. Deglaze using white wine.

Add the vegetable or chicken stock and potato then season with salt and pepper and simmer for five minutes.

Now using a slotted spoon, add the vegetables into hot jars about ¾ full then add stock and make sure that you leave an inch headroom. Use a wooden chopstick to get rid of air bubbles and adjust the headspace as required.

Wipe the rims with a cloth dampened with vinegar, place lid on jar and put the ring then tighten.

Place jars in pressure canner and process at 10 lbs pressure for weighted gauge canners for 40 minutes.

Turn off the heat and wait until the pressure drops to zero then open the lid and wait for 15 minutes before you can place the hot jars on a towel lined tray or counter to cool.

Potato Leek Soup
Yield: 6 half pints

Ingredients

6 potatoes

4 cups beef or chicken stock

5 lbs leeks, washed, soaked and sliced in a ¼ inch slices

6 half pint jars

Instructions

Peel and cube the potatoes and soak in cold water until ready to use. Put a bottom layer of leeks in the jar then add a layer of potatoes and finally a layer of leeks.

Add boiling hot chicken stock to fill the jars leaving an inch headroom. Ensure that you get rid of the air bubbles using a rubber spatula and then finally fill with additional stock until 1 inch headspace is left.

Process the rest of the vegetables in the same way in the other jars.

Once complete, process the jars in pressure canner at 11 pounds for 60 minutes for pints. If using quarts, process for 75 minutes.

Once the time elapses, place on a towel-lined tray to cool.

Canned Vegetables

Herbed peas

Ingredients

1 ½ to 3 lbs peas per pint

Thyme

Chervil

Water

Instructions

Wash the peas thoroughly. Drain, shell peas and wash again.

Place the peas in a pan and cover with boiling water for five minutes. Drain, rinse in hot water and drain again.

Put the hot peas in jars leaving one-inch headspace. Add ¼ teaspoon thyme, ¼ teaspoon chervil to each pint jar and ½ teaspoon thyme and ½ teaspoon chervil to each quart jar. Ladle the boiling water over the peas ensuring to leave an inch headspace. Ensure that you get rid of any bubbles, put the lid at the center of the jar and apply the band until adequately tight.

Process the jars in a pressure canner at 10 lbs pressure for 40 minutes.

Remove jars to cool, then check lids for seal after 12-24 hours.

Canned Carrots
Yield: 1 pint

Ingredients

1 ½ lb carrots

Water

Salt

Glass jars with lids and bands

Instructions

Wash and peel the carrots then wash again and cut carrots into slices or you can leave whole.

Pack the carrots into jars making sure that you leave an inch headspace and add around a teaspoon of salt to every quart jar if necessary.

Put hot boiling water over the carrots, ensuring you leave 1 inch headroom. You may use a wooden chopstick to get rid of any air bubbles, center lid on the jar then put the band and tighten.

Process the jars filled with carrots in a pressure canner at 10 pounds pressure and 25 minutes for pints.

Remove jars and cool then check the seal after 24 hours.

Carrots and Peas with Chives

What you will need

1 lb carrots per pint jar

1 lb peas in pods per pint jar

Boiling water

Salt

Jars with lids

Instructions

Prepare your pressure canner, then wash and drain the shell peas. Wash and peel the carrots then cut into ½-inch slices.

Combine the carrots and peas in a pan and cover with boiling water. Bring to a boil and boil for five minutes.

Pack the hot vegetables into jars making sure that you leave ½ inch head space. Add one teaspoon salt into every quart jar and ½ teaspoon salt into each pint jar or as desired. Add a tablespoon of snipped chives into every pint jar.

Ladle hot boiling water over vegetables and ensure that you leave an inch headspace. Remove the air bubbles, wipe the rim and center a hot lid on jar then put the band and adjust appropriately.

Process the filled jars in a pressure canner at 10 pounds pressure for 40 minutes for pints. Remove the jars and cool then check for seals after 24 hours. Ensure that the lid does not flex up and down when you press it at the center.

Conclusion

Thank you again for purchasing this book!

I hope this book was able to help you get started with canning and preserving your favorite foods. I also hope that you enjoyed the recipes as well and hope you love them as much as I do.

The next step is to start exploring with the recipes and see which one becomes your favorite.

Please check out my other books in this series as well to compliment what you have learned in this book. I have included a free preview of the next book in this series on the next page for your viewing pleasure. It is called *"Couponing For Beginners-How To Be A Savvy Shopper And Save Thousands A Year By Couponing.*" In this book I will teach you how to be a savvy shopper and save hundreds or even thousands of dollars each year by couponing.

Thanks!

Alex Wild

Preview Of 'Couponing For Beginners'

Our Innate Desire To Save

We all want to get the best deals for whatever items we buy. The reasoning here is simple; we want to get the most value for the least amount of money. Money is scarce; we simply don't have lots of luxury for spending it whichever way we want. Even the richest guys on earth want to buy stuff at a bargain. Or have you seen anyone asking for the price to be hiked before he or she can buy something? We simply don't have the luxury of paying more for anything because our reasoning is that there ought to be a way of getting it at a considerably lower price. Actually, you are bound to feel shortchanged if you buy any product only to discover that a friend bought it at a fraction of the price you paid for that product! Or would you be celebrating for paying more? Even if you were buying a luxury product, you still want to get the feeling that you got the best deal for that product; there is satisfaction in knowing that you paid the least possible price for anything you bought.

So, how do you get to a point of getting the best prices for whatever you are buying? The answer is pretty much simple; you have to deliberately search for the hottest deals in your locality or online if you are to take advantage of such deals. This isn't about hopping from one store to the next looking for products that have the label "buy one get one free". Although this could be considered a way of saving, you really cannot consider this couponing. Think about it, would you compare the "buy one get one free" buyer with someone who is buying a $100 priced product for $0.50? You probably have watched the "Extreme Couponing" TV show that showcases people who save thousands of dollars a year by buying products priced at several hundred dollars for less than a dollar and just wonder how someone could pull something of that magnitude. You might also have been stuck behind an extreme couponer for who bought loads of stuff only to pay a small fraction of what you paid for despite you having shopped for a minute fraction of the items he or she had shopped for. This should have gotten you wondering how someone could afford to buy all the stuff for such insanely low prices. The answer to this is simple; they used coupons to get insanely low prices. So, where do they get these coupons from? Couponing isn't just a cost saving measure but a hobby for some people.

It needs systematic approach and planning in order to derive the most benefits; if you are to be the shopper that saves 50-90% of your grocery bills every month, you really have to move from being an ordinary shopper who chooses a few coupons daily and throws away the others especially those that don't look appealing to them. Obviously, if you are new to couponing, you might find it tedious and time consuming to clip hundreds of coupons every week and even have an idea of where to start and where each of the coupons is. Couponing isn't about creating the most clutter in your home by cleaning the shelves! This book will walk you through the world of organized couponing so that you can make the most of your money; in any case, it's your money! Before we go into the details of how to collect coupons and how to make the most from couponing, let's first understand how couponing works so that you can have a clear picture of what you are getting yourself into:

What is a coupon?

A coupon is just a cash equivalent in that when you cut them from newspapers, magazines or get them online, the store you take it to will probably give you a discount on selected products. For instance, if you have a $5 off coupon on a pair of shoes, the cashier takes the coupon as if it were cash, which means that you won't pay $5 on specific shoes. What happens to the coupon after you have redeemed it is not your responsibility! The reasoning here is simple; manufacturers want to get people to buy their products, which is why they use the coupons to entice people to buy their selected products. This could be described to as a way of driving sales given that many of us would jump into any opportunity of getting something for unusually high discounts. Coupons are simply free money, which we all love!

Coupons are targeted to those who are fairly price sensitive such that they would probably buy something else or buy it elsewhere just to have a price reduction. In other words, they are a price discrimination strategy that manufacturers use to attract the price sensitive consumers who form a big proportion of every economy!

Perhaps, it is paramount that we understand the two broad types of coupons.

Types of coupons

#1 Store coupons

When a store issues coupons that are only redeemable in that particular store, these are referred to as store coupons. In this case,..............

© Copyright 2014 by Symbol LLC - All rights reserved.

This document is geared towards providing exact and reliable information in regards to the topic and issue covered. The publication is sold with the idea that the publisher is not required to render officially permitted, accounting, or otherwise, qualified services. If advice is necessary, legal or professional, a practiced individual in the profession should be ordered.

- From a Declaration of Principles which was accepted and approved equally by a Committee of the American Bar Association and a Committee of Publishers and Associations.

In no way is it legal to reproduce, duplicate, or transmit any part of this document in either electronic means or in printed format. Recording of this publication is strictly prohibited and any storage of this document is not allowed unless with written permission from the publisher. All rights reserved.

The information provided herein is stated to be truthful and consistent, in that any liability, in terms of inattention or otherwise, by any usage or abuse of any policies, processes, or directions contained within is the solitary and utter responsibility of the recipient reader. Under no circumstances will any legal responsibility or blame be held against the publisher for any reparation, damages, or monetary loss due to the information herein, either directly or indirectly.

Respective authors own all copyrights not held by the publisher.

The information herein is offered for informational purposes solely, and is universal as so. The presentation of the information is without contract or any type of guarantee assurance.

The trademarks that are used are without any consent, and the publication of the trademark is without permission or backing by the trademark owner. All trademarks and brands within this book are for clarifying purposes only and are the owned by the owners themselves, not affiliated with this document.

Manufactured by Amazon.ca
Bolton, ON